FUN BIBLE TALES

ABOUT

Learning to Trust in God

FUN BIBLE TALES ABOUT Learning to Trust in God

Yes, You Can, Moses!
The Brave But Gentle Shepherd
Good Sam
A Strange Place to Sing

A Happy Day® Books Gift Collection

Illustrated by Andy Stiles

*An Inspirational Press Book
for Children*

First Inspirational Press edition published in 1999.

Inspirational Press
A division of BBS Publishing Corporation
386 Park Avenue South
New York, NY 10016

Inspirational Press is a registered trademark of BBS Publishing Corporation.

Published by arrangement with The Standard Publishing Company,
8121 Hamilton Avenue, Cincinnati, OH 45231.

Library of Congress Catalog Card Number: 98-75456

ISBN: 0-88486-231-3

Designed by Coleen Davis

Printed in Mexico.

Yes, You Can,
Moses!

by
SANDY BROOKS

When Moses went closer to get a better look, he heard a voice say, "Moses, Moses! I am God."

Moses hid his face. He was afraid.

"Life is hard for my people in Egypt," God said.
"So I am sending you to the king.
Go, and bring my people out of Egypt!"
"I can't do that, God," said Moses.
"Yes, you can, Moses," said God.
"Just follow me and do what I say."

"Please ask someone else, Lord," said Moses. "I'm not a good talker. I just can't do it."

"Yes, you can, Moses," said God. "Just follow me and do what I say. And I will send your brother Aaron to help you."

Aaron met Moses in the desert,
and together they went to Egypt
to see the king.

Moses and Aaron saw the king.
"Let God's people go!" they told him.
But the king said, "God who?
I don't know your God.
And I will not let the people go."

Then the king made the people work harder than ever. And the people cried out to Moses. "I told you I couldn't do this, God," said Moses.

But God said, "Yes, you can, Moses. Just follow me and do what I say."

Because the king would not
let the people go,
God sent trouble to Egypt —
first, water they could not drink,

then frogs,

then gnats,

then flies,

then sickness,
then hail,
then locusts,
then darkness during the day,
and even death.

And finally the king said, "GO!"

So God's people quickly gathered up everything they needed and started on their journey.

But after the people left,
the king changed his mind.

"After them!" he cried,
and with his army
he chased God's people
all the way to the sea.

When God's people
saw the army coming,
they were afraid.

"We're trapped!" they cried.
"The sea is in front of us,
and the king's army is behind us!"

"I told you I couldn't do this, God," said Moses.

"Yes, you can, Moses," said God.
"Just follow me and do what I say.
Hold your walking stick over the sea."

**Moses did
what God said.**

All night long,
God sent a strong wind to part the sea.
All night long,
God held back giant walls of water
and his people walked across the sea
on dry ground.

The king and his army tried to follow
God's people into the sea.

But God let go of the walls of water,
and king and his army drowned.

Then Moses and the people sang
a song of praise to God.

"There's no one like you, God," said Moses. "And now I know I can do anything you ask, if I just follow you and do what you say."

I can do all things through Christ
because he gives me strength.
Philippians 4:13

The Brave but Gentle Shepherd

1 Samuel 17:34-37 retold by
TERRY WHALIN

**"You are my God,
and I will thank you."**

Psalm 118:28

In the little town of Bethlehem
in the country of Israel
lived a young shepherd boy.

David watched over a flock
of sheep for his father.

In the daytime, David found good grass
for the sheep to eat . . .

and cool, clean water for them to drink.

At night, David counted his flock to make sure every sheep had come home.

Then he built a fire to keep
wild animals away.

Whenever the sheep were sleepy and full,
they lay down to rest near David.
They felt safe beside their gentle shepherd.

Sometimes a small lamb wandered
away from the flock, chasing a butterfly.

Then David took the crook of his walking stick
and guided the lamb back to its mother.
"There, little one, don't wander off!" said David.

"Stay nearby where I can see you. Then you won't get into trouble." David swooped up the lamb and gave it a squeeze. The lamb's soft wool felt nice against his face.

While the sheep were grazing and resting, they could hear David strumming his harp and singing. David's songs were full of praise to God.

He thanked God for the sun that warmed his back in the day. He thanked God for the moon, so big and round in the starry sky.

He thanked God for taking care of him just as a shepherd cares for his sheep. David's songs were like a wonderful gift that David gave to God. He sang them over and over to the Lord.

David was gentle, but he was also brave. He was always ready to protect his sheep from danger.

Sometimes when the sheep were resting, David practiced throwing stones with his sling.

One afternoon, David was singing his songs
while the sheep lay around him, resting.
Suddenly, at the edge of the flock, the sheep
began bleating, "BAA! BAAA!"

David put down his harp.
"What's wrong with the sheep?" he wondered.
David put a stone in his sling as he looked
around the field. Then he saw —

A BEAR!

The bear had a lamb in its powerful arms and was dragging the lamb away for supper.

"BAAA!" cried the lamb.

Though David was young, he wasn't afraid.

"God, help!" he quickly prayed as he ran toward the bear.

Then he threw the stone in his sling with all his strength.

ZING!

The stone hit the bear right between the eyes.

The bear fell to the ground and dropped the little lamb.

David and the little lamb were safe!

David hugged the little lamb.
"Thank you, God," he said. "I knew you would help me. You are always with me."

Brave but gentle, David put his trust in God.

Good Sam

Jesus' Story of the Good Samaritan

based on Luke 10:25-37
retold by GLENDA PALMER

"Who is my neighbor?"
Jesus told a story to help us all understand that
our neighbor is anyone who needs *our* help . . .

Once there was a man
who went on a long journey all by himself.

He walked along, whistling a song,
when all of a sudden
robbers jumped out from behind a big rock!

The robbers took the man's clothes,
beat him up, and left him lying in the road.

The man felt *so-o-o* sad
and *shivering* cold,
and he *ached* all over,
from head to toe.

A selfish man on his way to town
came walking down the road.

He saw the hurt man,
so-o-o sad
and *shivering* cold,
and *aching* all over,
from head to toe.

The selfish man said,

"That poor man needs my help,
but I am on my way to town."

So he did not help.
Instead, the selfish man crossed over
to the other side of the road,
went on his way to town,
and never thought about
the hurt man again.

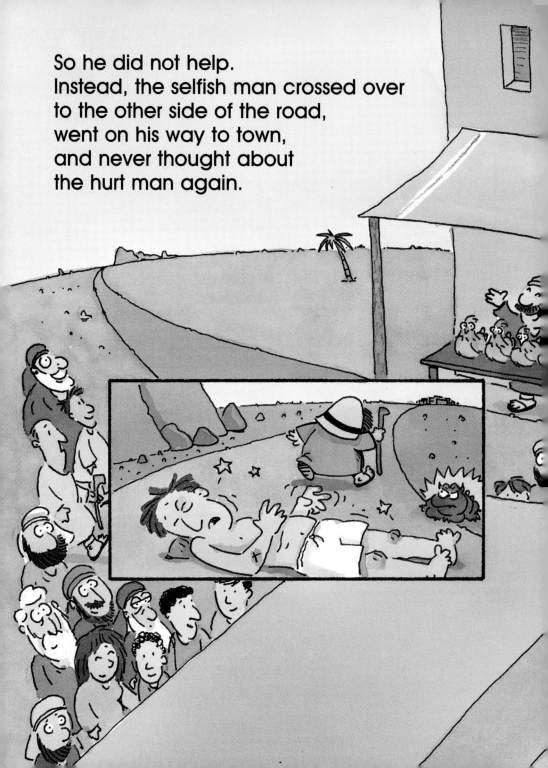

The selfish man was *not*
a good neighbor.

Then a proud man on his way to town came walking down the road.

He saw the hurt man, *so-o-o* sad and *shivering* cold, and *aching* all over, from head to toe.

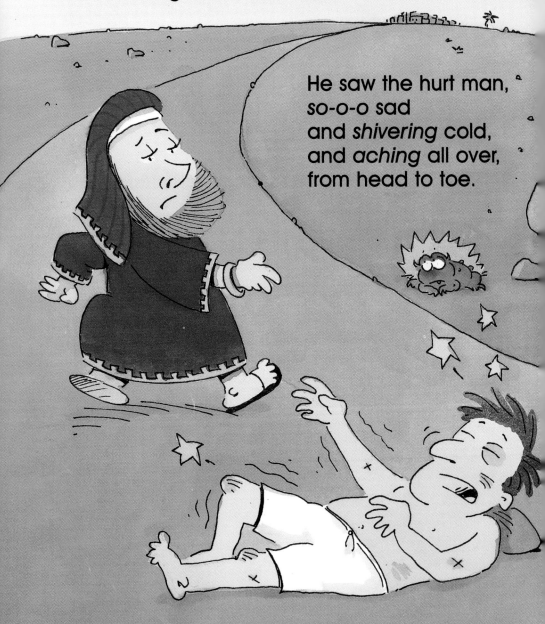

The proud man said,

"This poor man needs my help,
but I am on my way to town."

So he did not help.

Instead, the proud man crossed over
to the other side of the road,
went on his way to town,
and never thought about
the hurt man again.

The proud man was *not*
a good neighbor.

Then Good Sam, from another country,
came riding down the road.
Sam was not selfish. Sam was not proud.

Sam saw the hurt man,
so-o-o sad
and *shivering* cold,
and *aching* all over,
from head to toe . . .

and Sam felt sorry for him.

"This poor man needs my help!"
said Sam.

So Sam stopped to help.

First Sam covered the poor shivering man with his own warm coat. And the man said, "Thank you very much."

He washed the man's cuts
and put bandages on them.
And the man said,
"You are very kind."

Then Sam put the man on his own donkey and took him to a place where he could eat and sleep and get well.

And Good Sam paid for it all!

"Which of these three was a neighbor to the man who was hurt?" asked Jesus.

Not the selfish man.

Not the proud man.

Good Sam was the good neighbor, because *he* helped!

"I want *you* to be just like Good Sam!" said Jesus.

A Strange Place to Sing

written by
TERRY WHALIN

Paul and Silas were in big-time trouble . . .

The problem began when Paul and Silas
came to the town of Philippi.
They were telling people about Jesus, God's Son.

But some people didn't like Paul and Silas. These men said Paul and Silas were doing bad things — even though they weren't.

The men hauled Paul and Silas before the judges of the town.

"These two should be in jail," the men said. "We don't like what they are doing."

The crowd shouted, "Yeah. Toss them into jail!"

"We agree," said the judges. "Take them away and lock them up!"

The soldiers beat Paul and Silas
and dragged them off to prison.

"Guard these men carefully,"
they told the jailer.
"If they escape, it will be your fault."

The jailer took
Paul and Silas
deep into
the prison.

Paul and Silas were alone.
It was too dark to see anything.
Their bodies hurt,
and they couldn't move.

The other prisoners were surprised.
They listened to every word.
Even in the middle of the night,
Paul and Silas were still praying and singing,
praising God.

The prisoners' chains rattled and fell off, and all the doors popped open.

When the shaking stopped,
the jailer ran in and saw all the open doors.
My prisoners have escaped! he thought.
I am in terrible trouble now.
The jailer pulled out his sword.

The jailer couldn't believe it.
He called for a light.
Then he dropped on his knees
in front of Paul and Silas.
"I heard you singing," he said.
"How can I be saved?"

"Believe on the Lord Jesus," said Paul and Silas.
"Then you will be saved, and your whole family."

The jailer did believe in Jesus.
His family did too.
Paul and Silas baptized them all.

Then, with great joy,
everyone ate a meal together.

In the morning, the judges let Paul and Silas go.

"But you must leave our town," the judges said.

Paul and Silas said good-bye to the jailer and his family.

Then they left, happy that God had used their singing — even in a very strange place!